SAY GOODBYE TO YOUR SOUTHERN ACCENT

A DO-IT-YOURSELF GUIDE TO CHANGING THE WAY YOU SPEAK

BOOK & AUDIO CD SET

JENNIFER ADAMS, M.ED., CCC-SLP &
JOHANNA CHAPMAN, M.ED., CCC-SLP

LANGUAGE SUCCESS PRESS

ANN ARBOR, MICHIGAN

Credits: The map on page 4 was adapted with permission from an original map
by Robert Delaney.

First Edition
Printed in the United States of America

ISBN: 978-0-9817754-3-2

Bulk discounts are available. For information, please contact:

Language Success Press
2232 S. Main Street #345
Ann Arbor, MI 48103
USA

E-mail: sales@languagesuccesspress.com
Fax: (303) 484-2004 (USA)
www.languagesuccesspress.com

ACKNOWLEDGEMENTS

A special thank you to our families for their never-ending support, and to our fellow speech-language pathologists for holding down the fort at Atlanta Accent Management, LLC while we worked on this book. Thank you to Sindy Nicholls for lending her voice to the audio recording.

ABOUT THE AUTHORS

Jennifer Adams and Johanna Chapman are managing partners at Atlanta Accent Management, LLC. Jennifer and Johanna hold Master's degrees in Speech Language Pathology from the University of Virginia and are certified speech-language pathologists (CCC-SLP). They are members of the American Speech Language Hearing Association and are certified in the specialization of Accent Reduction through the Institute of Language and Phonology in San Francisco, California.

TABLE OF CONTENTS

I. INTRODUCTION

Congratulations on taking a giant step toward modifying the way you speak! You are about to see just how easy it is to do, and the results will be life-changing. *Say Goodbye to Your Southern Accent: A Do-it-Yourself Guide to Changing the Way You Speak* provides a systematic and comprehensive plan for reducing your Southern accent. It doesn't matter which Southern state you are from or whether your "accent" is mild or heavy...the results will be big!

Let experts Jennifer Adams and Johanna Chapman, owners of a successful accent reduction practice in the South, guide you through your transformation. Adams and Chapman are certified speech-language pathologists. Their techniques are:
- Easy-to-follow
- Effective
- Comprehensive: the program addresses pronunciation, lexicon, and grammar
- Personalized: the program takes into account a variety of Southern dialects
- Tailored to allow you to work at your own pace and come back for review as often as needed

At the end of your study, you will have achieved:
- An understanding of the components that create your "accent"
- A Standard American English dialect
- Increased confidence in professional and social settings
- Decreased fears of being pre-judged or stereotyped

Say Goodbye to Your Southern Accent will enable you to achieve your communication goals. Now that you have the right tools, get ready for rapid success. You'll be amazed at what you can do!

II. SPEECH PATTERNS OF THE SUNNY SOUTH

So, you want to reduce your Southern "Accent?"...
You've come to the right place!

Perhaps you do business with people from other regions and have experienced difficulty in communicating because of your Southern drawl. Or maybe you are preparing for a job in a field where a "neutral" accent is beneficial, like news broadcasting or acting. Perhaps you have felt pressure from the prejudice and stereotyping that goes along with the Southern "accent." Whatever the reason, there are a few things you should know.

First, an "accent" is only a part of how we speak. Since an accent is simply defined as "the way speech sounds are pronounced," this term leaves out a lot of critical information. Instead, the more comprehensive word "dialect" should be used. "Dialect" refers to sound pronunciation (accent), and also includes lexicon and grammar. People who speak a Southern dialect have differences in the way they pronounce sounds, the vocabulary and expressions they use (lexicon), and in their grammar. Therefore, from now on we will use "Southern dialect" to refer to the way in which you speak.

Second, a "neutral accent" is nonexistent. Whether you're from the North or South, East or West, you speak a dialect — from the Californian "yo dude," to the Northern "yous guys," and down to the Southern "y'all," there is simply no getting around it.

The main dialects in the United States fall into the following general groups: Northern, Midwestern, Western, and Southern. There are several subcategories within these groups. You may then wonder what it is you are working towards?!? Well, the most common American English dialect is the "Standard American English" dialect. It's considered a standard because of its historical association with social groups that were considered prestigious and because it is the most widespread dialect in the USA.

It's typically spoken in the Midwest and on the West Coast and is the dialect used in dictionary transcriptions. When we think of people we consider "accentless," such as many newscasters, it is the Standard American English dialect we are hearing. Therefore, the goal of this program is to help you acquire a Standard American English dialect.

The dialect we speak results from how, where, and when we learned English. The main influence on the way we speak English dates back to our childhoods. It has come from the people around us, certainly including our parents and other family members, but even more so from the people we "cut up with" — our friends and schoolmates. Our dialects can be altered over a lifetime depending on where we live and with whom we spend time, so even though most of us have a primary dialectal influence on our speech, we probably have a combination of two or more dialects shaping the way we speak today. Finally, a dialect does not indicate intelligence or competency despite the stereotypes, which we know all too well. Again, any dialect follows its own rules of pronunciation, lexicon, and grammar. These rules may differ from the rules of other dialects, but that does not make them improper or less correct. The Southern American dialect is a recognized version of the English language in its own right.

Where did the Southern dialect come from...?
The Southern dialect dates back to the 1700's, when Celtic settlers came to the area. The Celtic influence, combined with the influence of African American English, created the general Southern dialect. Of course, Celts were not the only settlers in the South. Since the infusion of settlers differed notably from one area of the South to another, several subcategories of the Southern dialect exist. A perfect example of this would be the large settlement of the French in areas like New Orleans, where Creole (a subcategory of the Southern dialect) exists.

Where are you from? Where are some other places you've lived? We're able to identify the influences on our speech by considering these factors. It's important to identify this information because, while there are many common characteristics among the Southern dialects, there are also differences in all three areas (pronunciation, lexicon, and grammar). Let's consider this example: General Southern dialect is known for dropping the [r] sound after vowels ("butter" becomes "buttuh"), but speakers from the South Midland area of Appalachia actually add the [r] to words where it is not considered standard ("wash" becomes "warsh").

This map shows the different Southern dialects. Where do you fit in?

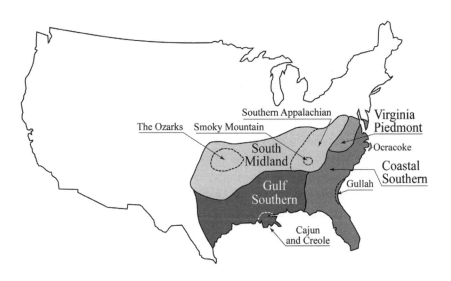

III. "FIXIN' TO" START THE PROGRAM

Now that you have some background on the Southern American dialect and have identified which area of the South has most impacted your speech, you're ready to begin the transformation!

When changing the way you speak, practice makes perfect. Furthermore, the way you practice determines your success. This program features an easy-to-follow format. Let's go over a few points before getting started:

1. This program offers an all-inclusive approach to changing your Southern dialect. It includes target sound lessons with activities to address pronunciation issues and additional lessons to tackle other important dialectal concerns. All lessons are presented in a specific order to maximize learning. *Please complete all lessons in the order provided from front to back!*

2. Each target sound lesson corresponds to a track on your audio CD. The audio CD is a key part of your learning experience. *Please use the audio CD while working through this program.*

3. At the beginning of each target sound lesson, you will see one or more notes indicated by a "Don't Forget" symbol. These are

DON'T FORGET...

the concepts to be applied to each lesson. They refer to all Southern dialects, unless otherwise noted. In some instances, there are pointers to apply if you are from a certain area. In others, you will discover that you can skip a chapter completely. *Pay attention to the "Don't Forget" notes!*

4. While working on the lessons, your goal is twofold:
   a. Practice with your text and audio CD. *We recommend working on only two lessons at a time. You should always skip at least a day before beginning your next two lessons.* This will ensure that you have achieved carryover of what you have learned.
   b. Work on carrying over your skills into your everyday conversational speech.

5. ***Follow our 40-minute formula for practice.*** Use the program text and audio CD for 20 minutes per day and practice your new skills an additional 20 minutes using our carryover strategies *(see pages 8-10).*

6. Each target sound lesson is organized by hierarchy, with each step building upon the other. ***Do not jump around. Work through each target sound chapter thoroughly and in the steps provided!*** There are four levels of content in the text and on the audio CD. You'll reach your ultimate goal at Level 5, when you're able to use your target sounds in everyday conversations.

Let's review how to work through each of the five levels in detail...

LEVEL 1: LISTENING SECTION(S)

Listening is the foundation of changing the way you speak. In order to change your pronunciation, you must be able to identify the difference between your own pronunciation and that of a Standard American English speaker. Listening sections first present the Southern pronunciation of your target sound, followed by the Standard American English pronunciation of the same word. Some lessons have an additional listening section, designed to help you discriminate between the target sound and a sound commonly substituted. These sections are clearly marked. Your goal with both types is to listen closely to the audio CD to identify the difference between them.

Take your time with these activities. Use the audio CD to listen and repeat the word pairs aloud two to three times. Pause your audio CD as needed. Work on them until you are confident in your ability to discriminate.

LEVEL 2: WORD SECTION

These word lists are not exhaustive by any stretch of the imagination, but represent a range of commonly used words. The target sound in the example word is bolded, providing a visual cue.

Use the audio CD to listen and repeat each word aloud while applying the "Don't Forget" concepts noted at the top of each chapter. Complete the exercise by mimicking the vocal model at least three times. When you are confident in your ability to repeat target words, move on.

LEVEL 3: SENTENCE SECTION

These sentences are loaded with words that contain your target sound and, once again, the target sound is bolded to provide a visual cue.

Use the audio CD to listen and repeat aloud the sentences while applying the "Don't Forget" concepts noted at the top of each chapter. Complete the exercise by mimicking the vocal model at least three times. Break the sentence down into a few phrases if you are having trouble with it. Once you feel you have mastered the target sentences, move on.

LEVEL 4: PARAGRAPH SECTION

The final step in each target sound chapter is the paragraph section. The target sounds in the paragraph are bolded, providing a visual cue.

Use the audio CD to listen to the paragraph one time through from beginning to end. Once you have listened to the paragraph in its entirety, work through the paragraph sentence by sentence, pausing your audio CD at each period in order to practice repeating. Then try putting them all together and read the paragraph without stopping. Practice reading the paragraph at least three times.

LEVEL 5: CARRYOVER INTO CONVERSATION

It will not be very helpful if you can speak Standard American English only while you're working with this program. We want you to be able to speak without being asked where you're from, give a presentation without worrying about how you're being perceived, and converse naturally using your new skills. Folks, carryover of your new skills into everyday conversation is the whole reason you are here! *Carryover practice should begin the minute you start working through the program, and should be continued well after you are through.* Again, aim for 20 minutes of this type of practice each day. Focus on your newest target sounds and/or dialectal goals while also keeping in mind what you have already learned from past lessons. At any point, you may choose to go back and focus on carryover of a specific technique or sound that you found challenging.

Make sure that each target sound and goal has had at least a day or two of focused carryover practice. And, it never hurts to take an extra day or two of carryover practice before moving on to new information.

To figure out the best way to incorporate carryover practice into your daily life, ask yourself:

- What type of learner am I? Visual? Auditory?
- Which types of activities can be easily incorporated into my already busy day?

Once you have answered these questions, use some or all of the suggestions below to integrate carryover practice into your daily routine:

☑ Establish visual cues in your environment to remind yourself to use your new skills. For example, place Post-it notes in strategic places (on your computer keyboard, on your phone, in your car....) to remind you to pay close attention to your speech for a few minutes here and there.

☑ Mentally associate a specific person or a room with your new pronunciation. Concentrate on your speech when you see this person or enter this room.

☑ Read aloud from newspaper or magazine articles, focusing on your pronunciation.

☑ Read incoming or outgoing email messages aloud from time to time.

☑ Listen to nationally televised news and radio programs for what is typically an excellent model of the Standard American English dialect (hint: avoid Nancy Grace!). You can learn a lot from listening to neutral speakers. Try repeating the headlines using your new skills.

☑ Focus when you are on the telephone. It can be an outstanding practice tool!

☑ Add carryover practice to your "to do" list or planner, or set your cell phone to alert you to practice your new skills.

☑ If you love your MP3 player, download the tracks from your audio CD onto your device and get some additional listening and repeating time in while you're on the go!

☑ Record yourself using your new skills in words and/or sentences you use often. Listen to yourself and critique your performance. (A hand-held digital voice recorder or old-fashioned cassette recorder will do the trick. To take the more high-tech route, buy a headset microphone and download free software for recording from Audacity: http://audacity.sourceforge.net/).

7. One of the main differences between Southern and Standard American pronunciation is in vowel length. Southern American English speakers make vowels considerably longer than speakers of Standard American English. You'll have the opportunity to hear this difference in vowel length while working through the listening sections of the target vowel sounds, but now that we've pointed it out, we bet that you can already identify it in your own speech.

We will repeatedly refer to the process of reducing vowel length. We call it "Vowel Reduction Technique" — or "VRT" — *and VRT is the golden key to changing your Southern speech!* The best part is that VRT is nothing fancy....it is simply as it implies, "making the vowel shorter." For some people, using the upcoming consonant in a word as a cue to "cut off" the vowel works wonders. And please "don't worry your pretty little head" about making a vowel *too* short....we hear that concern a lot, but we assure you that it doesn't hurt to pronounce the sounds a bit too short while working through the word sections. Then, miraculously, once you're speaking in connected speech (sentences, paragraphs, conversation), it all takes care of itself.

8. Finally, remember that in this program each lesson builds on previous lessons. *Once you've completed a target sound or dialectal goal, you are officially responsible for it!* That means we assume you've mastered it and will be using your new speech skills from then on. Try applying sounds from previous lessons

to the lesson you are currently studying. The concepts from sound to sound are similar, so managing this is less painful than it may sound!

In Summary:

✓ *Complete all lessons in the order provided from front to back!*

✓ *Use the audio CD while working through each target sound activity.*

✓ *Pay close attention to the "Don't Forget" notes!*

✓ *Follow our 40-minute formula: 1. Practice 20 minutes a day using the text and the audio CD and 2. Spend 20 minutes a day on carryover practice.*

✓ *Do not attempt to work on more than two new lessons at a time, and skip AT LEAST ONE DAY between starting the next new lessons!*

✓ *Do not jump around. Work through each target sound lesson thoroughly, deliberately, and in the steps provided!*

✓ *Be sure to understand how to work through each of the four levels (Listening, Words, Sentences, Paragraphs) before you begin.*

✓ *Carryover practice should begin the minute you start working through the text, and should be continued well after you are through.*

✓ *VRT is the golden key of changing your Southern speech!*

✓ *Once you have addressed a target sound or dialectal goal, you are responsible for it!*

IV. WHAT DO THOSE SYMBOLS MEAN?
The IPA

Don't let the symbols confuse you...

As you begin working through the target sound lessons, you'll notice the use of a symbol system called the International Phonetic Alphabet, or IPA. The IPA is a tool for transcribing the speech sounds of any language.

Although at first glance the IPA may look complex, it actually simplifies the pronunciation of sounds in a language. **With the IPA, each sound has its own symbol.** This isn't the case with the English alphabet. Let's consider the English alphabet letter "A".

Pronounce each word out loud.

English Word	English Alphabet Letter	IPA Symbol
Mad	A	æ
Father	A	a
Late	A	e

Notice how each English alphabet "A" sounds different, but is represented by the same symbol? The IPA takes the confusion out by assigning a different symbol to each of the different sound pronunciations.

How this relates to you...

This program focuses mainly on pronunciation of vowel sounds. However, we've listed both the IPA vowel and consonant symbols. These symbols are here for your reference since they are used throughout the text. You do not need to memorize them.

IPA Consonant Symbols			
p	pig, top	s	sit, pass
b	boy, web	z	zoo, has
t	take, it	ʃ	shoe, wash
d	dog, mad	ʒ	measure, beige
tʃ	chew, beach	h	ham, hello
dʒ	joy, edge	m	money, lamb
k	cat, back	n	never, pen
g	give, dig	ŋ	going, being
f	face, calf	l	light, ball
v	verb, have	r	rat, run
θ	think, math	w	we, wash
ð	this, bathe	j	yellow, yes

IPA Vowel Symbols			
æ	after, happy	e	late, day
a	father, on	ɛ	bet, said
ʌ	cup, of	ɚ	her, better
ɪ	in, sit	ʊ	look, put
i	heat, each	u	food, new
o	go, code		

IPA Diphthong Symbols			
aɪ	sky, mine	iɚ	hear, deer
ɔɪ	oil, toy	oɚ	more, four
aʊ	house, now	eɚ	fair, where
ju	you, few	aɪɚ	tire, buyer
aɚ	car, start	aʊɚ	power, sour

accent   Pronunciation of the sounds of a language.

articulation   The formation of speech sounds produced from the use of "articulators" (lips, tongue, teeth, and jaws).

carryover   The process of applying the concepts taught throughout this program into everyday conversational speech.

demonstrative adjective   An adjective that points out which person, object or concept you are referring to (examples: this hat, that book, those children, these people).

dialect   A regional and/or social variety of a language that includes variations in the three main areas of sound pronunciation (accent), lexicon, and grammar.

diphthong   The combination of two vowels to form one sound unit.

elongate   To make long or stretch out.

International Phonetic Alphabet (IPA)   A tool for transcribing the speech sounds of any language, in which each sound has its own symbol.

lax vowel   A vowel made with mostly relaxed tongue muscles in contrast to the tense vowels.

lexicon   Vocabulary, expressions, or arrangement of words in a sentence that is characteristic of a specific dialect.

modal verb   A verb that provides additional information about the mood of the main verb (examples: will, shall, may, might, would, can, could, must, should, ought to).

multi-syllabic words   Words with multiple "units." See "syllable."

nasal consonant   Consonants produced in the nasal cavity (/n/, /m/ and /ŋ/).

neutralize To simplify or not pronounce a sound completely.

reflexive verb A verb in which the subject and the object of the action are the same.

Southern dialect(s) or Southern American English A dialectal region that includes Alabama, Georgia, Tennessee, Mississippi, North Carolina, South Carolina, Louisiana, and Arkansas. It also includes southern and eastern Oklahoma, southern West Virginia, the Ozark areas of Missouri, and the Florida Panhandle.

speech-language pathologist A specialist who evaluates and treats communication differences and disorders.

Standard American English dialect A dialect that is used as a standard because it is the most common and widespread dialect, and also because of its historical association with social groups who were viewed as prestigious.

syllable A unit of speech made up of a vowel or vowel-consonant combination.

tense vowel A vowel made with the tongue muscles relatively more tense than a lax vowel.

Vowel Reduction Technique (VRT) The technique of shortening vowel length.

word stress The emphasized syllable of a word.

VI. THE LESSONS

PHASE 1:
VOWELS

LESSON 1
Vowel /i/

DON'T FORGET...

...that the main difference between Southern and Standard American pronunciation of all vowels, including vowel /i/,* is vowel length. While working on vowel /i/, focus on applying VRT (shorten the length of the vowel!).

DON'T FORGET...

...to pay special attention to /i/ at the ends of words. Southern American English speakers tend to replace /i/ with /ɛ/. For example, "hurry" becomes "hurreh." Take care to pronounce the /i/ with force!

LEVEL 1: LISTENING

The italicized words represent Southern pronunciation

Seen – Seen	*She* – She
Team – Team	*Even* – Even
Need – Need	*Money* – Money

* /i/ is considered a tense vowel. Tense vowels can often times be considered diphthongs and can also be written /iy/.

1. **Each**
2. Team
3. Clean
4. Keep
5. Deal
6. She
7. Tea
8. Speak
9. Keys
10. Please
11. Week
12. Agree
13. Coffee
14. **Easy**
15. Create
16. **Money**
17. Meeting
18. Complete
19. Guarantee
20. Company
21. Increase
22. Employee

1. A **tea**m has been assigned to create an agenda.
2. She speaks to her mother **each** week.
3. Complete this form to transfer the mone**y**.
4. Would you like **tea** or coff**ee**?
5. Our **dea**l was that you **keep** your room clean.
6. Do you ag**ree** with the company policy?
7. Ple**as**e make three cop**ies**.
8. It was **ea**sy to agree on a meeting place.
9. There is no guarant**ee** that w**e** will incre**as**e our sales this year.

The employ**ee** was having a bad w**ee**k. On Monday, **she** was late because **she** lost her ke**ys**. On Tuesday, **she** was too busy to complete her research for the three o'clock **tea**m meeting. Later in the w**ee**k, **she** spilled **tea** on her compan**y** computer and then lost a big **dea**l that was supposed to be a guarantee. By Friday, **she** was read**y** to spe**ak** with her boss about taking a personal lea**ve**.

...that the main difference between Southern and Standard American pronunciation of all vowels, including vowel /ɪ/, is vowel length. In the case of /ɪ/, the elongation of the vowel is so extreme that it actually becomes two syllables linked by a "yuh" sound.

DON'T FORGET...

Elongated example:
/ɪ/ becomes /ɪ/ + "yuh" = "this" becomes "thi/yuhs"

While working on vowel /ɪ/, your goal is to shorten the sound to ensure that it is only pronounced as one syllable. Focus on applying VRT and do not add "yuh."

...that in Southern American English, the vowel /ɪ/ is often pronounced the same as the vowel /ɛ/ when it comes before a nasal consonant (/m/, /n/, and /ŋ/). For example, "pen" and "pin" sound the same. This occurs in all areas of the South, with the exception of New Orleans and Savannah. If you're from anywhere else, use the listening activities below to hear the difference between /ɪ/ and /ɛ/, and practice the /ɪ/ and /ɛ/ sections with the goal of differentiating between these two sounds.

DON'T FORGET...

...to review special notes pertaining to words with asterisks on this page. These notes are in the "Level 2: Words" section.

DON'T FORGET...

Pin – Pen   *Been* – Ben
Tin – Ten   *Lint* – Lent
Him – Hem   *Trimmer* – Tremor

LEVEL 1B: LISTENING

The italicized words represent Southern pronunciation

Sit – Sit   *Middle* – Middle
With – With   *Income* – Income
Give – Give   *Office* – Office

LEVEL 2: WORDS

1. Is	11. Will	21. Office
2. In	12. Build	22. Ethics
3. Did	13. Different	23. Finish
4. Been	14. Budget	24. Possible
5. With* (not wif)	15. Middle	25. Limit
6. Bill	16. Invest	26. Business**
7. Sick	17. Income	27. Internet
8. Give	18. Traffic	28. Decision
9. Print	19. Inside	29. Competition
10. Risk	20. Credit	30. History

* Take care if you are from South Midland (including Appalachia and the Ozarks) to avoid pronouncing Final /θ/ as /f/.

** All Southern American English speakers should take note of words with /z/ before /n/, as it is common to change the /z/ to /d/. For example, "budiness" instead of "business." Other examples include the words "hasn't" and "wasn't."

1. The sky is the limit.
2. The competition was stiff.
3. I need your decision as soon as possible.
4. Will you please give me my bill?
5. She will fill out the application on the Internet.
6. He is in the insurance business.
7. I have been sitting in traffic for an hour.
8. The office assistant was sick.
9. We took a risk by investing in that company.

LEVEL 4: PARAGRAPH

There is a great deal of risk associated with building a new business. It's an adventure that will take each individual down a different path. Many factors need to be considered, including: budgets, income, competition, office location, and inventory. A lot of work is involved, but business ownership can bring many rewards. You will never know if you can do it if you don't give it a try!

LESSON 3
Vowel /e/

...that the main difference between Southern and Standard American pronunciation of all vowels, including vowel /e/,* is vowel length. While working on vowel /e/, focus on applying VRT!

DON'T FORGET...

LEVEL 1: LISTENING

The italicized words represent Southern pronunciation

Day – Day   *Able* – Able
Late – Late   *Okay* – Okay
Save – Save   *Safety* – Safety

LEVEL 2: WORDS

1. **Pay**
2. Take
3. Same
4. Page
5. W**ait**
6. Make
7. Late
8. S**ay**
9. Change
10. **Eigh**t /Ate
11. Paper
12. Alw**ays**
13. Mond**ay**
14. Safety
15. Training
16. Favorite
17. Mistake
18. Replace
19. Educate
20. Communicate

* /e/ is considered a tense vowel. Tense vowels can often times be considered diphthongs and can also be written /eɪ/.

1. We always get paid on Friday.
2. Are we all on the same page?
3. It's never too late to say "I'm sorry."
4. Filing insurance claims gives me a headache.
5. I'd appreciate it if you'd save me a seat at the table.
6. I made a mistake on the paperwork.
7. Someone from the agency came on Tuesday.
8. We need to change the way we operate.
9. Can we change the date of the training?

The retail company is planning a training program for the week of May eighth. As a travel agent, I'm in charge of making arrangements. First, I have to book plane reservations to San Diego. Then I'll arrange a car to take the employees to the Holiday Inn. I'll also make requests for late check-in and make sure that everyone will be staying on the same floor. I'm taking pains to look after all the details, so hopefully everything will go okay.

LESSON 4
Vowel /ɛ/

 ...that the main difference between Southern and Standard American pronunciation of all vowels, including vowel /ɛ/, is vowel length. In the case of /ɛ/, the elongation of the vowel is so extreme that it actually becomes two syllables linked by a "yuh" sound.

DON'T FORGET...

> Elongated example:
> /ɛ/ becomes /ɛ/ + "yuh" = "head" becomes "hea/yuhd"

While working on vowel /ɛ/, your goal is to shorten the sound to ensure that it is only pronounced as one syllable. Focus on applying VRT and do not add "yuh."

 ...that, in Southern American English, the vowel /ɛ/ is often pronounced the same as the vowel /ɪ/ when it comes before a nasal consonant (/m/, /n/, and /ŋ/). For example, "pen" and "pin" sound the same. This occurs in all areas

DON'T FORGET...

of the South, with the exception of New Orleans and Savannah. If you're from anywhere else, use the listening activities below to hear the difference between /ɛ/ and /ɪ/, and practice the /ɛ/ and /ɪ/ sections with the goal of differentiating between these two sounds.

LEVEL 1A: LISTENING TO THE DIFFERENCE BETWEEN /ɛ/ AND /ɪ/

When – Win   *Tent* – Tint
Ken – Kin   *Meant* – Mint
Gem – Gym   *Jen* – Gin

The italicized words represent Southern pronunciation

Bed – Bed	*Test* – Test
Let – Let	*Second* – Second
End – End	*Weather* – Weather

LEVEL 2: WORDS

1. Best
2. **Said**
3. Let
4. Sell
5. Debt
6. Check
7. **End**
8. Well
9. Men
10. Test
11. Send
12. **Extra**
13. Collect
14. **Penny**
15. Letter
16. Credit
17. Second
18. Internet
19. Depend
20. Agenda
21. Eleven
22. Recommend

LEVEL 3: SENTENCES

1. I recommend that you follow the agenda.
2. The seller wanted top dollar for the development.
3. Our Internet connection is down.
4. Our revenue grew twenty percent this year.
5. I received the letter via express mail.
6. We will sell to the person who makes the best offer.
7. Please send me a check for the rent.
8. She would benefit by settling the debt.
9. The weather better improve for the outdoor benefit.

LEVEL 4: PARAGRAPH

The end of the month is always hectic at work. Departments depend on each other to send month-end reports; agendas must be set for upcoming events. Payroll needs to be double-checked and sent to accounting. Finally, all pending files must be collected, edited, and uploaded to the Internet. If everything goes well, the next month tends to get off to a better start.

LESSON 5
Vowel /æ/

DON'T FORGET... ...that the main difference between Southern and Standard American pronunciation of all vowels, including vowel /æ/, is vowel length. In the case of /æ/, the elongation of the vowel is so extreme that it actually becomes two syllables linked by a "yuh" sound.

Elongated example:
/æ/ becomes /æ/ + "yuh" = "that" becomes "tha/yuht"

While working on vowel /æ/, your goal is to shorten the sound to ensure that it is only pronounced as one syllable. Focus on applying VRT and do not add "yuh."

LEVEL 1: LISTENING

The italicized words represent Southern pronunciation.

Had – Had   *Happy* – Happy

Ask – Ask   *Accent* – Accent

Back – Back   *Contract* – Contract

LEVEL 2: WORDS

1. As*
2. That*
3. Have*
4. Staff
5. Cash
6. After
7. Plan
8. Value
9. Back
10. Tax
11. Dad
12. Asset
13. Adapt
14. Cancel
15. Average
16. Traffic
17. Factor
18. Advertise
19. Calendar
20. Balance
21. Application
22. Analysis

* The 'a' in "as," "that," "have," and "can" is pronounced /æ/ only when these words are stressed (emphasized).

1. You can't improve your **accent** if you don't practice!
2. What is the value of all your **assets**?
3. They **asked** me to come **back** after lunch.
4. Can you **fax** me the contract?
5. We have to cancel our family vacation.
6. **Half** of the **staff** was late for the meeting due to traffic.
7. You have to **ask** the **administrator** for **access** to the computer.
8. The presentation **lacked valuable** information.
9. I have to renew my cell phone plan.

I can't believe I lost my job at the event **planning** company! I got along well with my **manager and** was really **happy**. Maybe this is my chance to better use my **academic** training in **ad**vertising. Tomorrow I will **fax** my résumé and **application** to companies that would be a good **match**. I'm optimistic about my new plan. **After** all, things **happen** for a reason, and I know I'll **add value** to any **staff**.

...that the main difference between Southern and Standard American pronunciation is the tendency to "neutralize" (not pronounce completely) the /r/ sound. *Your main goal with vowel /ɚ/ is to pronounce the /r/ with force!*

...that the other difference between Southern and Standard American pronunciation of all vowels, including vowel /ɚ/, is vowel length. *While working on this sound, focus on applying VRT!*

...that /r/ is typically not a concern if you are from South Midland (including Appalachia and the Ozarks). People from these areas even go so far as to add /r/ where it is not considered standard. For example, "warsh" for "wash." Take care to avoid doing so, and skip these /r/ sections unless you feel that practice may be beneficial.

LEVEL 1: LISTENING

The italicized words represent Southern pronunciation.

Her – Her	*Learn* – Learn
Earn – Earn	*Better* – Better
Word – Word	*Over* – Over

1. Work
2. Firm
3. Learn
4. Word
5. Term
6. Earn
7. Merge

8. Were
9. After
10. Early
11. Lower
12. Perfect
13. Over
14. Number

15. Journal
16. Purchase
17. Director
18. Interview
19. Standard
20. Supervisor

1. There is a lot of turnover at that firm.
2. The director earned the top sales award.
3. I will purchase a new computer.
4. The research was published in a journal.
5. The printer has run out of paper.
6. Our manager is a superb public speaker.
7. The first quarter numbers looked good.
8. Ernst & Young is the sponsor of Thursday's event.
9. We will follow standard procedure after the merger.
10. Our supervisor prefers that we come into work early.

Yesterday, Peter interviewed for an opening at the firm. He heard about the opportunity in the "Daily News Journal," and was looking forward to learning more about the position. When he arrived, he met first with the department supervisor to talk about his résumé and review his work history. Before leaving, he sat down with the financial director to discuss benefits and go over numbers. A week later, he received a job offer letter.

LESSON 7
Vowel /ʌ/

...that the main difference between Southern and Standard American pronunciation of all vowels, including vowel /ʌ/, is vowel length. While working on vowel /ʌ/, focus on applying VRT!

DON'T FORGET...

...to review special notes pertaining to words with asterisks. These notes are in the Level 2: Words section.

DON'T FORGET...

LEVEL 1: LISTENING

The italicized words represent Southern pronunciation.

Us – Us   *Money* – Money
Does – Does   *About* – About
Sun – Sun   *Discuss* – Discuss

LEVEL 2: WORDS

1. The*	11. Agree	21. Product
2. Of	12. Money	22. Upload
3. Us	13. Under	23. Continue
4. Was	14. Income	24. Opinion
5. Some	15. Account	25. Approach
6. Does	16. Support	26. Suddenly
7. Month**	17. Company	27. Agenda
8. Budget	18. Public	28. Reasonable
9. About	19. Number	29. Affiliated
10. Enough	20. Refund	30. Reduction

* The word "the" is pronounced "thuh" when it is comes immediately before a word starting with a consonant. It is pronounced "thee," when it comes immediately before a word starting with a vowel.
** Take care if you are from South Midland (including Appalachia and the Ozarks) to avoid pronouncing Final /θ/ as /f/.

---

1. What is on today's agenda?
2. The meeting on product design is on Monday.
3. The luggage was held up at customs.
4. What is the premium for that much coverage?
5. Tech support will help us upload the new program.
6. The public showed support for the judge.
7. Funding for college is available through public programs.
8. How much money is in the trust fund?
9. After much discussion, they agreed to disagree.

Professional athletes earn an exceptional income, but the work can be tough. Athletes are under pressure to keep their bodies in great condition. Their agenda is full of so many practice sessions, games, and public appearances that they aren't home much. There is a lot of pressure from the public to perform well each season. No wonder most retire young!

LESSON 8
Vowel /u/

DON'T FORGET... ...that the main difference between Southern and Standard American pronunciation of all vowels, including vowel /u/,* is vowel length. While working on vowel /u/, focus on applying VRT!

LEVEL 1: LISTENING

The italicized words represent Southern pronunciation

Do – Do   *Lose* – Lose

Knew – Knew   *Approve* – Approve

Soon – Soon

LEVEL 2: WORDS

1. To**
2. Do/Due
3. Knew
4. Lose
5. Soon
6. Rule
7. Group
8. Choose
9. Noon
10. School
11. Approve
12. Reduce
13. Remove
14. Overdue
15. Revenue
16. Newspaper
17. Consumer
18. Attitude

* /u/ is considered a tense vowel. Tense vowels can often times be considered diphthongs and can also be written /uw/.

** The 'u' in "to" is pronounced /u/ when the word is stressed (emphasized) or followed by a word beginning with a vowel.

1. Did he choose to vote on the issue?
2. I am walking* to lunch with a group of co-workers at noon.
3. We are past the statute of limitations to sue.
4. Consumer spending fluctuated during the third quarter.
5. Are you doing enough to reduce global warming?
6. We went on a cruise in lieu of getting a new pool.
7. The lieutenant's platoon is due back in June.
8. Do not lose the chance to invest in this lucrative opportunity.

* Southern American English speakers tend to pronounce /l/ in words where it is considered "silent." Common examples include the words: walk, talk, calm, and salmon. Take care to avoid pronouncing the /l/ in these words.

A group of students met at noon to write the first issue of their school newspaper. They'd finally gotten approval for the project from the superintendent two days ago. The students knew that they would have to work hard to prove that the project would benefit the school. They planned to write about local news, post reviews of cafeteria food, and keep people informed of new rules. They couldn't wait to get started. This newspaper was long overdue!

DON'T FORGET... …that the main difference between Southern and Standard American pronunciation of all vowels, including vowel /ʊ/, is vowel length. While working on vowel /ʊ/, focus on applying VRT!

LEVEL 1: LISTENING

The italicized words represent Southern pronunciation

Put – Put	*Should* – Should
Look – Look	*Input* – Input
Good – Good	*Wouldn't* – Wouldn't

LEVEL 2: WORDS

1. Look
2. Would / Wood
3. Foot
4. Cook
5. Good
6. Push
7. Put
8. Could
9. Book
10. Stood
11. Woman
12. Sugar
13. Outlook
14. Useful
15. Helpful
16. Shouldn't
17. Careful
18. Thoughtful
19. Bulletin
20. Beautiful

1. Could you please have a look at this document?
2. I don't think you should put up with that.
3. Could you help me get my foot in the door?
4. Books on managing your money are helpful.
5. He should be able to pull it off.
6. The outlook for the fourth quarter is good.
7. The cook put together a wonderful meal.
8. The news bulletin warned that bad weather would be coming.
9. My kids eat cookies by the handful.

LEVEL 4: PARAGRAPH

Kelly is in charge of preparing the baked goods for her women's book club meeting tonight. Kelly's mother, who is a wonderful cook, once taught her how to make the family's famous sugar cookies. She looked and looked for the recipe her mother had given her, but to be truthful she may have thrown it away. She really should've been more careful! It's been a while since she made them herself, so hopefully she'll be able to pull it off. She trusts her memory, but it'll be embarrassing if they don't taste good.

DON'T FORGET...

...that the main difference between Southern and Standard American pronunciation of all vowels, including vowel /o/,* is vowel length. While working on vowel /o/, focus on applying VRT!

LEVEL 1: LISTENING

The italicized words represent Southern pronunciation

Go – Go   *Phone* – Phone

Hope – Hope   *Open* – Open

Close – Close   *Total* – Total

LEVEL 2: WORDS

1. No
2. Own
3. Close
4. Loan
5. Code
6. Show
7. Home
8. Slow
9. Over
10. Total
11. Notice
12. Social
13. Open
14. Promote
15. Stolen
16. Postage
17. Radio
18. Motivate
19. Proceeds
20. Negotiate
21. Notification
22. Protocol

* /o/ is considered a tense vowel. Tense vowels can often times be considered diphthongs and can also be written /oʊ/ or /ow/.

1. The shareholders spoke on the telephone.
2. You have to go to the bank to get a loan.
3. The logo on the brochure looks good.
4. All proceeds will go to charity.
5. I need postage for this envelope.
6. The broker explained the pros and cons of lowering the cost of our home.
7. The goal was to motivate local businesses to promote their services.
8. We hope no one will protest the decision to build a new road.

Having your identity stolen is no joke. Last week I was notified that I had overdrawn my bank account. I was concerned, so I decided to probe further. After going over my account details, I spoke with my credit card company and discovered that I was caught up in a hoax. They said my ATM code may have been stolen or that someone may have opened an envelope that was confidential. I will now have to notify the credit report agencies and follow their protocol to regain control over my finances!

LESSON 11
Vowel /a/

 DON'T FORGET... ...that the main difference between Southern and Standard American pronunciation of all vowels, including vowel /a/, is vowel length. While working on vowel /a/, focus on applying VRT!

LEVEL 1: LISTENING

The italicized words represent Southern pronunciation

On – On   *Option* – Option
Job – Job   *Dollar* – Dollar
Got – Got   *Process* – Process

LEVEL 2: WORDS

1. Not
2. A lot
3. Stop
4. Job
5. Clock
6. Box
7. Got
8. Profit
9. Copy
10. Option
11. Forgot
12. Doctor
13. Conflict
14. Operate
15. College
16. Process
17. Hospital
18. Deposit
19. Positive
20. Holiday
21. Economy
22. Approximately
23. Occupation
24. Document

1. I forgot to turn off my desktop.
2. She has a positive attitude and is very cooperative.
3. The month of December has a lot of holidays.
4. Please drop the deposit off at the bank by 5 o'clock.
5. The company will be modifying their stock option plan.
6. A copy of the economic forecast was in today's column.
7. She got a job at the top hospital in Washington.
8. He has the option to drop the class by October 30th.

LEVEL 4: PARAGRAPH

After weighing many options, Tom Rogers decided to become a doctor. Despite his father's concern that being a doctor might stop him from having a quality personal life, he went on to medical school. Currently, Doctor Rogers works at the local hospital and performs approximately ten operations a day. Although he works around the clock, including most holidays, the idea of making a positive contribution to society keeps him optimistic. He may have had a lot of possible career options, but he's confident that he chose the right occupation!

PHASE 2:
VOWEL COMBINATIONS & CONSONANTS

LESSON 12
Diphthong /ju/

...that a diphthong is the combination of two vowel sounds.

DON'T FORGET...

...that the main difference between Southern and Standard American pronunciation of all vowels, including diphthong /ju/, is length. While working on diphthong /ju/, focus on applying VRT!

DON'T FORGET...

LEVEL 1: LISTENING

The italicized words represent Southern pronunciation.

Use – Use	*Argue* – Argue
Few – Few	*Value* – Value
Menu – Menu	*Music* – Music

LEVEL 2: WORDS

1. **You**	10. Dispute	19. Annual
2. **Few**	11. Nephew	20. Distribute
3. Used	12. Usual	21. Interview
4. Unit	13. United States	22. Graduate
5. Argue	14. Uniform	23. Community
6. Future	15. Popular	24. Occupation
7. Menu	16. Document	25. January
8. Review	17. Computer	26. Individual
9. Excuse	18. Regular	

1. The music in your cubical is too loud!
2. A pink diamond is of great beauty and value.
3. Let's review our results in January.
4. The executive retreat is in Munich this year.
5. I like that restaurant because the menu items are so unusual.
6. The university computer classes are very popular.
7. My nephew has a unique sense of humor.
8. Please distribute the memo congratulating Mrs. Smith on her humanitarian award.
9. Communities must regulate water usage during a drought.

LEVEL 4: PARAGRAPH

The executive committee has scheduled a meeting in January for the annual review of company policies to discuss these issues:
- Universal rules for settling billing disputes
- New guidelines for interviewing
- Annual sales volume goals
- Rules for continuing education units

All new procedures will be printed in the revised company manual. This document will then be distributed to all U.S.-based units.

...that the main difference between Southern and Standard American pronunciation of all vowels, including diphthong /ɔɪ/, is length. While working on diphthong /ɔɪ/, focus on applying VRT!

DON'T FORGET...

LEVEL 1: LISTENING

The italicized words represent Southern pronunciation.

Boy – Boy   *Oyster* – Oyster

Join – Join   *Enjoy* – Enjoy

Noise – Noise   *Avoid* – Avoid

LEVEL 2: WORDS

1. Toy
2. Oil
3. Void
4. Joint
5. Noise
6. Boy
7. Voice
8. Joy
9. Coin
10. Choice
11. Spoil
12. Point
13. Foyer
14. Boycott
15. Loiter
16. Oyster
17. Toilet
18. Annoy
19. Avoid
20. Voyage
21. Exploit
22. Invoice
23. Enjoy
24. Loyal
25. Destroy
26. Ointment
27. Disappoint
28. Employee

1. He enjoys collecting coins.
2. Avoid buying toys containing lead.
3. We enjoyed the PowerPoint presentation.
4. In the turmoil, he forgot he had an appointment.
5. Our new employee will join us for the meeting.
6. The boy got poison ivy while digging in the soil.
7. If he's not loyal, you should avoid entering a joint venture with him.
8. The disappointed union members made the choice to boycott the meeting.

Ben starts off his Sundays by reading the "Detroit Voice." Making headlines this week was the disappointing increase in oil prices. One customer reported avoiding filling her tank by joining with friends to carpool. In international news, the turmoil in Iraq was at a minimum thanks to an additional convoy of deployed troops. The tabloid section of the paper reported the joint venture of two well-known Hollywood stars on an upcoming film about a cowboy's voyage through the Wild West. After reading the paper cover to cover, Ben was ready to enjoy his day.

LESSON 14
Diphthong /aʊ/

...that the main difference between Southern and Standard American pronunciation of all vowels, including diphthong /aʊ/, is length. While working on diphthong /aʊ/, focus on applying VRT!

DON'T FORGET...

...to review special notes pertaining to words with asterisks. These notes are in the Level 2: Words section.

DON'T FORGET...

LEVEL 1: LISTENING

The italicized words represent Southern pronunciation.

How – How   *Power* – Power

Down – Down   *About* – About

Loud – Loud   *Flower* – Flower

LEVEL 2: WORDS

1. **Out**	10. **Down**	19. Acc**ount**
2. **Now**	11. **Cow**	20. With**out**
3. **South***	12. **Noun**	21. Disc**ount**
4. **How**	13. **Ground**	22. Pron**ounce**
5. **Loud**	14. **Crowd**	23. Th**ou**sand
6. **Town**	15. **Found**	24. Backgr**ound**
7. **Shout**	16. Am**ount**	25. H**ow**ever
8. **Count**	17. **Power**	26. F**ou**ndation
9. **House**	18. **About**	

* Take care if you are from South Midland (including Appalachia and the Ozarks) to avoid pronouncing Final /ө/ as /f/.

---

1. The accounting firm will be downsizing.
2. Only a thousand people live in that tiny town.
3. The executive council met to announce the new CEO.
4. The discount was applied without our knowledge.
5. The foundation held the ceremony outside.
6. The forecast is for partly cloudy skies with a chance of showers.
7. Lori found a brown scarf at the store downtown.
8. Accountants put in countless hours during tax season.

LEVEL 4: PARAGRAPH

After Jeff and Stephanie's kids left the house for college, they decided to downsize. They had always wanted to live downtown and, without a houseful of kids, they felt that now was the time. Stephanie had a few requirements: something close to town, a deck to plant her flowers, and a master bedroom with a large shower. On Saturday, they looked at what seemed like a thousand condos! They finally found one that had everything they wanted without a steep price. Although they have no doubt about their decision to move, Jeff and Stephanie are not looking forward to the hours and hours of packing. Somehow it'll all get done!

...that the main difference between Southern and Standard American pronunciation of all vowels, including diphthong /aɪ/, is length. While working on diphthong /aɪ/, focus on **DON'T FORGET...** applying VRT!

 ...that a diphthong is the combination of two vowel sounds to create one sound unit. The combination of vowel /a/ + vowel /ɪ/ creates the /aɪ/ diphthong. Practice saying the /a/, **DON'T FORGET...** then the /ɪ/. Then, combine them quickly to create /aɪ/. The Southern American English pronunciation of /aɪ/ is strongly characterized by leaving off the /ɪ/. Be sure to pronounce both sounds!

LEVEL 1: LISTENING

The italicized words represent Southern pronunciation.

Sky – Sky	*Rely* – Rely
Nice – Nice	*Item* – Item
Mine – Mine	*Final* – Final

LEVEL 2: WORDS

1. Mine	9. Life	17. Beside
2. Five	10. **High**	18. **Goodbye**
3. Try	11. Decide	19. Financial
4. Line	12. Friday	20. Notify
5. Size	13. Client	21. Exercise
6. Find	14. Inside	22. Arrival
7. **Buy/By**	15. Apply	23. Society
8. Right/Write	16. Behind	24. Apologize

1. I apologized for arriving late.
2. Let's apply the rules of supply and demand.
3. The handwriting on that file is not mine.
4. If the company does not reply to the demands, there will be a picket line.
5. The right client will meet the asking price.
6. The highest bidder at the silent auction won the prize.
7. My flight will arrive in China at nine o'clock tonight.
8. Jim will provide you with an update on the company finances by five o'clock.

Vicki has been working for an advertising agency in Providence, Rhode Island since nineteen ninety-nine. The clients were so demanding and the hours so tiring, that in early July she notified her supervisor that she was resigning. While she was exercising at the gym last Friday, she saw a poster advertising a five-week guided tour to Ireland. She bought a ticket leaving on July nineteenth and left a voice mail notifying callers that she would return calls upon her arrival home. After she makes a few final arrangements and finds a ride to the airport, she will be organized and on her way.

… that the main difference between Southern and Standard American pronunciation is the tendency to "neutralize" (not pronounce completely) the /r/ sound. Your main goal with diphthong /iɚ/ is to pronounce the /r/ with force!

…that the other difference between Southern and Standard American pronunciation of all vowels, including diphthong /iɚ/, is vowel length. While working on this sound, your other goal is to focus on applying VRT!

…that /r/ is typically not a concern if you are from South Midland (including Appalachia and the Ozarks). Speakers from these areas even go so far as to add /r/ where it is not considered standard. For example, "warsh" for "wash." Take care to avoid doing so, and skip these /r/ sections unless you feel that practice may be beneficial.

LEVEL 1: LISTENING

The italicized words represent Southern pronunciation.

Ear – Ear	*Fierce* – Fierce
Near – Near	*Steer* – Steer
Deer – Deer	*Career* – Career

1. **Ear**
2. Hear/**Here**
3. **Y**ears
4. Near
5. Fear
6. **Dear/Deer**
7. Cheer
8. **Beer**
9. Peer/**Pier**
10. Gear
11. **Pierce**
12. Steer
13. **Fierce**
14. Smear
15. Sphere
16. Beard
17. Weird
18. Career
19. Hearing
20. **Irritate**

1. Many y**ear**s ago, Aristotle proved that the Earth was a sph**ere**.
2. New Y**ear**'s Eve is a ch**eer**ful occasion.
3. **Here** are the documents for tomorrow's h**ear**ing.
4. The hikers packed plenty of rain g**ear** to battle the fi**er**ce storm.
5. My high school counselor tried to st**eer** me away from a car**eer** in fashion.
6. In the winter months, pediatricians see a lot of kids with **irr**itat-ing **ear** infections.
7. My grandmother was f**ear**ful that her **irr**egular heart beat was due to a hereditary disease.

Despite her fi**er**ce f**ear** of traveling by plane, Cathy will be joining her p**eer**s on a trip to the coast for New Y**ear**'s. She decided that she could not miss out on the trip after h**ear**ing the details of the rental house by the p**ier** with the private pool n**ear**by. She can't wait to ch**eer**fully ring in the New Y**ear** with her d**ear**est friends. She feels ready to face her f**ear** of flying!

LESSON 17
Diphthong /eɚ/

 …that the main difference between Southern and Standard American pronunciation is the tendency to "neutralize" (not pronounce completely) the /r/ sound. Your main goal with diphthong /eɚ/ is to pronounce the /r/ with force!

 …that the other difference between Southern and Standard American pronunciation of all vowels, including diphthong /eɚ/, is vowel length. While working on this sound, your other goal is to focus on applying VRT!

 …that /r/ is typically not a concern if you are from South Midland (including Appalachia and the Ozarks). Speakers from these areas even go so far as to add /r/ where it is not considered standard. Take care to avoid doing so, and skip these /r/ sections unless you feel that practice may be beneficial.

LEVEL 1: LISTENING

The italicized words represent Southern pronunciation.

Air – Air   *Marry* – Marry
There – There   *Carrot* – Carrot
Where – Where

1. **Air**/**Heir**
2. There/Th**eir**
3. Wh**ere**/W**ear**
4. P**air**/P**ear**
5. Sh**are**
6. F**air**/F**are**
7. R**are**
8. H**air**
9. Pray**er**
10. V**ary**
11. C**are**ful
12. Hardw**are**
13. M**arry**
14. N**arrow**
15. P**arent**
16. Somewh**ere**
17. Silverw**are**
18. Gu**ar**antee
19. App**ar**ently
20. Prim**ary**
21. Everywh**ere**
22. Libr**ary**

1. Appa**ar**ently, the softw**are** was installed incorrectly.
2. She likes to w**ear** her h**air** short.
3. The U.S. milit**ary** occupies that foreign t**err**itory.*
4. The libr**ar**ian told me that the diction**ar**ies were somewh**ere** by the encyclopedias.
5. I gu**ar**antee you that the gen**er**ic* form of that drug is very effective.
6. Bryce proposed m**arr**iage to his girlfriend with the two-c**ar**at diamond ring he inh**er**ited* from his grandmother.
7. Brandon donated a p**air** of r**are** coins to an Am**er**ican* charity.

The thought of animal h**air** getting everywh**ere** had kept me from getting a dog. Once I got m**arr**ied and became a p**arent**, my kids talked me into it. At first, we considered adopting a Labrador Retriever, but appa**ar**ently they shed more than th**eir** f**air** sh**are**! After considering v**ar**ious other breeds, we chose a short-h**air**ed t**err**ier* through a local breeder. Recently, she ate a p**air** of my shoes. After that, we learned to be c**are**ful about what we leave around!

* The 'er' in bold in these words can also be pronounced as /ɛr/.

...that the main difference between Southern and Standard American pronunciation is the tendency to "neutralize" (not pronounce completely) the /r/ sound. Your main goal with diphthong /oɚ/ is to pronounce the /r/ with force!

DON'T FORGET...

...that the other difference between Southern and Standard American pronunciation of all vowels, including diphthong /oɚ/, is vowel length. While working on this sound, your other goal is to focus on applying VRT!

DON'T FORGET...

...that /r/ is typically not a concern if you are from South Midland (including Appalachia and the Ozarks). Speakers from these areas even go so far as to add /r/ where it is not considered standard. Take care to avoid doing so, and

DON'T FORGET... skip these /r/ sections unless you feel that practice may be beneficial.

LEVEL 1: LISTENING

The italicized words represent Southern pronunciation.

For – For   *Order* – Order
More – More   *Before* – Before
Your – Your   *Support* – Support

1. **Or**
2. F**or***
3. Y**our****
4. M**ore**
5. St**ore**
6. Sh**or**t
7. T**owar**d
8. **Or**der
9. Bef**ore**
10. Aff**ord**
11. Rep**ort**
12. Inf**orm**
13. F**or**eign
14. Supp**ort**
15. Perf**orm**
16. B**ored**
17. **Or**ganize
18. F**orm**ula
19. Pri**or**ity
20. Invent**ory**
21. C**or**poration
22. Auth**or**ity

1. Please **pour** me some **more** coffee.
2. I supp**ort** you in y**our** decision.
3. There is a sh**or**tcut to that file on your desktop.
4. After the st**or**m, we had to file a disaster claim f**orm**.
5. I have to memorize the f**or**mulas **for** the test.
6. Isabella will **or**der new flo**or**ing from that st**ore**.
7. Please **or**ganize the invent**ory** **for** the sale on Monday.
8. If you can't aff**ord** your m**or**tgage, you'll have to f**ore**close.

Austin has wanted to open a company for some time. His f**or**mer partner started a p**or**celain manufacturing plant in China **four** years ago and is now making a f**or**tune. Austin's top pri**or**ity is to set up a c**or**porate bank account. His next step is to look into the laws and regulations of imp**or**ting and exp**or**ting goods. Then he will need to **or**ganize a trip to China to find a location for the plant. In **or**der to prepare for his trip, he must get a passp**or**t from the post office. He is looking f**or**ward to this new opportunity!

* "For" is often pronounced "fer," especially when it is not stressed.
** "Your" is often pronounced "yer," especially when it is not stressed.

...that the main difference between Southern and Standard American pronunciation is the tendency to "neutralize" (not pronounce completely) the /r/ sound. Your main goal with diphthong /aɚ/ is to pronounce the /r/ with force!

DON'T FORGET...

...that the other difference between Southern and Standard American pronunciation of all vowels, including diphthong /aɚ/, is vowel length. While working on this sound, your other goal is to focus on applying VRT!

DON'T FORGET...

...that /r/ is typically not a concern if you are from South Midland (including Appalachia and the Ozarks). Speakers from these areas even go so far as to add /r/ where it is not considered standard. Take care to avoid doing so, and skip these /r/ sections unless you feel that practice may be beneficial.

DON'T FORGET...

LEVEL 1: LISTENING

The italicized words represent Southern pronunciation.

Are – Are	*Army* – Army
Far – Far	*Sorry* – Sorry
Start – Start	*Guitar* – Guitar

1. **Are**
2. **Car**
3. **Dark**
4. **Far**
5. **Arm**
6. **Part**
7. Start
8. Hard
9. March
10. **Farm**
11. Card
12. Smart
13. Carpet
14. Sorry
15. **Argue**
16. Apart
17. **Party**
18. Market
19. Alarm
20. Garbage
21. **Participate**
22. Kindergarten
23. Regarding
24. Pharmacy
25. Partnership
26. Sarcasm

1. My **car** won't start!
2. Alex is planning a large party for the end of **March**.
3. That doctor published an **article** on the harmful effects of artificial sweeteners.
4. **Are** you going to participate in the department meeting?
5. Target's new marketing campaign is very artistic.
6. My new apartment has a marvelous view of Central Park.
7. The charming cottage with the large backyard is on the market.
8. The parking garage gets very dark at night, so they hired a guard.

Barbara and Jeanne have been friends since kindergarten. Jeanne is working hard to plan a surprise party for Barbara's 40th birthday on March 9th. At first she was planning to have the party at her apartment, but then she decided on a charming restaurant on Park Street instead. She has included many of Barbara's favorite things: carnations, a variety of barbequed foods, and a large ice carving. She can hardly wait to see how startled her friend will be when she arrives at the restaurant on the night of the party!

LESSON 20
Diphthong /aɪɚ/

…that /aɪɚ/ is a diphthong. This diphthong adds three sounds: /a/ + /ɪ/ + /r/. One of the main differences between Southern and Standard American pronunciation is the tendency to "neutralize" (not pronounce completely) the /r/ sound. Another characteristic is completely leaving off the /ɪ/ in the /aɪ/ sound combination. Your main goal with diphthong /aɪɚ/ is to pronounce all three sounds with force!

DON'T FORGET…

…that the other difference between Southern and Standard American pronunciation of all vowels, including diphthong /aɪɚ/, is vowel length. While working on this sound, your other goal is to focus on applying VRT!

DON'T FORGET…

…that /r/ is typically not a concern if you are from South Midland (including Appalachia and the Ozarks). Speakers from these areas even go so far as to add /r/ where it is not considered standard. Take care to avoid doing so, and skip these /r/ sections unless you feel that practice may be beneficial.

DON'T FORGET…

LEVEL 1: LISTENING

The italicized words represent Southern pronunciation.

Tire – Tire   *Dryer* – Dryer
Wire – Wire   *Entire* – Entire
Fire – Fire   *Retire* – Retire

1. Hire	8. Choir	15. Supplier
2. Liar	9. Prior	16. Inspire
3. Wire	10. Flyer	17. Vampire
4. Tire	11. Buyer	18. Admire
5. Fire	12. Tired	19. Acquire
6. Pliers	13. Entire	20. Perspire
7. Dryer	14. Empire	21. Amplifier

1. Do you need pliers to change a tire?
2. I do not admire people who are liars.
3. Leaving the dryer on while not home is a fire hazard.
4. The entire church choir sang on Sunday.
5. Part of my job is to hire and fire employees.
6. Do you have any desire to read the book about vampires?
7. The flyer said to inquire about a discount.
8. Prior to being hired at the law firm, Jacob was a firefighter.

Prior to working in retail, Stephen acquired his degree from UCLA. He has been a buyer at a company in California for his entire career. Although he loves living out West, he has always had a desire to live on the East Coast before retiring. He inquired about a position at a clothing supplier when he heard that they were hiring for their Manhattan office. He thought he met the job requirements. He applied, was hired, and moved just two days later. He is now renting an apartment near the Empire State Building. Although he is tired from the move, he is excited to live and work in a city he has always admired.

LESSON 21
Diphthong /aʊɚ/

...that the main difference between Southern and Standard American pronunciation is the tendency to "neutralize" (not pronounce completely) the /r/ sound. Your main goal with diphthong /aʊɚ/ is to pronounce the /r/ with force!

DON'T FORGET...

...that the other difference between Southern and Standard American pronunciation of all vowels, including vowel /aʊɚ/, is vowel length. While working on this sound, your other goal is to focus on applying VRT!

DON'T FORGET...

...that /r/ is typically not a concern if you are from South Midland (including Appalachia and the Ozarks). Speakers from these areas even go so far as to add /r/ where it is not considered standard. Take care to avoid doing so, and skip these /r/ sections unless you feel that practice may be beneficial.

DON'T FORGET...

LEVEL 1: LISTENING

The italicized words represent Southern pronunciation.

Our – Our
Sour – Sour
Tower – Tower

Flower – Flower
Power – Power
Shower – Shower

1. **Our***/**Hour**
2. S**our**
3. C**owar**d
4. T**ower**
5. P**ower**
6. Sh**ower**
7. Fl**ower**/Fl**our**
8. D**owry**
9. Sc**our**
10. **Our**selves
11. Horsep**ower**
12. Sunfl**ower**
13. Emp**ower**
14. Caulifl**ower**

1. Do you like s**our** candy?
2. H**ow're** you today?
3. April sh**ower**s bring May fl**ower**s.
4. Meet me in the west t**ower** of the office building in an h**our**.
5. The p**ower** was out for two h**our**s after the storm.
6. **Our** boss sc**our**ed his office for the missing file.
7. In the Wizard of Oz, the c**owar**dly lion emp**ower**ed himself and overcame his fears.
8. Do you mind if we help **our**selves to some of your sunfl**ower** seeds?

Starting a garden is something H**owar**d and I decided to do **our**selves. Sure, we could have hired a landscaper for $50 an **hour**, but I thought it would be something fun for the whole family. We started off by renting a **power**ful tiller with high horsep**ower** to prepare the soil. Next, we planted a section for fl**ower**s, and a section for vegetables like tomatoes, carrots, and caulifl**ower**. After a long hot day in the sun, **our** next order of business was to take a sh**ower**!

* "Our" can also be pronounced /ar/.

LESSON 22
Consonant: Final /ŋ/

DON'T FORGET...

…that a common characteristic in the speech patterns of those who speak a Southern dialect is the simplification of the suffix /ŋ/ ("-ing"). Your goal when working /ŋ/ is to avoid pronouncing the end sound as "n." Instead, pronounce it as "ing," like in the word "sing."

Example:
Southern dialect: "I was runni**n**' late for the meeting."
Standard American English: "I was runni**ng** late for the meeting."

LEVEL 1: LISTENING

The italicized words represent Southern pronunciation.

Doin' – Doing   *Gettin'* – Getting
Talkin' – Talking   *Fixin'* – Fixing
Workin' – Working   *Helpin'* – Helping

LEVEL 2: WORDS

1. Do**ing**
2. Tell**ing**
3. See**ing**
4. Us**ing**
5. Fix**ing**
6. Pay**ing**
7. Div**ing**
8. Gett**ing**
9. Chang**ing**
10. Think**ing**
11. Look**ing**
12. Work**ing**
13. Beginn**ing**
14. Consider**ing**
15. Stand**ing**
16. Tak**ing**
17. Out**ing**
18. Buy**ing**
19. Send**ing**
20. Learn**ing**
21. Meet**ing**
22. Build**ing**
23. Help**ing**
24. Cloth**ing**
25. Increas**ing**
26. Organiz**ing**
27. Check**ing**
28. Park**ing**

1. Organiz**ing** and pay**ing** the bills is my job.
2. I was think**ing** about go**ing** on a vacation in May.
3. Are you bring**ing** a fruit salad to the company out**ing**?
4. The park**ing** garage attendant has been work**ing** since 8:00 a.m.
5. I will be send**ing** you a fax sometime this morn**ing**.
6. Build**ing** and maintain**ing** a strong financial portfolio is hard work.
7. The retail company was increas**ing** sales by offer**ing** more cloth**ing** lines.
8. Brad is help**ing** raise money for a local charity by host**ing** a cloth**ing** drive.

Nicole became interested in cloth**ing** design after attend**ing** a sew**ing** class last summer. Dur**ing** the six week class, Nicole began design**ing** a dress for her upcom**ing** wedd**ing**. As the class progressed, she kept improv**ing** her skills. At the end, Nicole's dress was stunn**ing**. After a stand**ing** ovation at the class graduation, she was consider**ing** go**ing** into a career as a fashion designer!

…that consonant /l/ can influence how vowels /e/ and /ɛ/ are pronounced. Southern American English speakers do not make the distinction between /e/ and /ɛ/ when they come before consonant /l/. Therefore, words such as "fail" and "fell" sound the same. Use the following activities to practice the difference between /e/ and /ɛ/ in words that end in /l/. Be sure to clearly pronounce each, with appropriate distinction between them.

DON'T FORGET…

…the same is true of the vowels /i/ and /ɪ/. Southern American English speakers do not make the distinction between /i/ and /ɪ/ when they come before consonant /l/. Therefore, words like "peel" and "pill" sound the same. Use the following activities to practice the difference between /i/ and /ɪ/ in words that end in /l/. Be sure to clearly pronounce each, making the appropriate distinction between them.

DON'T FORGET…

LEVEL 1A: LISTENING TO THE DIFFERENCE BETWEEN /e/ AND /ɛ/

Fail – Fell   *Whale* – Well
Sail – Sell   *Jail* – Gel
Tail – Tell   *Bail* – Bell

LEVEL 1B: LISTENING TO THE DIFFERENCE BETWEEN /i/ AND /ɪ/

Meal – Mill   *Heal* – Hill
Deal – Dill   *Wheel* – Will
Steal – Still   *Peel* – Pill

/e/ and /ɛ/

1. Fail   I hope you don't **fail** the test.
2. Fell   The stock market fell 10% today.

3. Sale   John put his house up for **sale**.
4. Sell   When will you **sell** your car?

5. Tail   That dog has a bushy **tail**.
6. Tell   Please **tell** him I said hello.

7. Jail   The county is building a new **jail**.
8. Gel   Mark doesn't use hair **gel**.

9. Bail   He has been a **bail** bondsman for twenty years.
10. Bell   The church **bell** sounded at noon.

/i/ and /ɪ/

1. Meal   I eat three **meal**s a day.
2. Mill   Susan passed me the pepper **mill**.

3. Heal   Hopefully her broken ankle will **heal** quickly.
4. Hill   Michael lives in Beverly **Hill**s.

5. Feel   How do you **feel** about your new position?
6. Fill   Please **fill** my water glass.

7. Deal   We closed the **deal** last Wednesday.
8. Dill   Do you like the taste of dill?

9. Peel   Please **peel** the banana.
10. Pill   When do you have to take your **pill**s?

/e/ and /ɛ/

Dale and Becky were packing to go on their summer vacation when Dale tripped and fell down the stairs. He broke his ankle and was not feeling well, but they did not want to bail on the trip of a lifetime. They were too excited about their plans of whale watching and catching sales at the local markets. Plus, think of all the tales they could tell of Dale's adventures on crutches!

/i/ and /ɪ/

Jill's catering business, Meals at the Mill, is in charge of food service for events at the newly renovated steel mill downtown. Business has been slow, but Jill just signed a deal to prepare the meal for the wedding of Anita Hill. The price of $30 per guest is a steal and includes roasted veal, dill potatoes, and peeled vegetables. The guests will get their fill of desserts too. Although she is still waiting for the first half of Ms. Hill's bill to be paid, Jill feels that things are looking up!

LESSON 24
The Importance of Word Stress:
INSURANCE vs. INSURANCE

Let's start with the basics...

A syllable is a unit of speech made up of a vowel or vowel-conso-nant combination. Words with multiple "units" are referred to as multi-syllabic words. Take a look at the following examples:

Word	Number of Syllables
At	1
Good-bye	2
Fan-tas-tic	3
Psy-chol-o-gy	4
Un-be-liev-a-ble	5

All multi-syllabic words have at least one syllable that is more emphasized, or "stressed," than the others. This is referred to as "word stress." In the following table, the stressed syllables are bolded:

Word	Number of Syllables
At*	1
Good-**bye**	2
Fan-**tas**-tic	3
Psy-**chol**-o-gy	4
Un-be-**liev**-a-ble	5

* Single syllable words are automatically stressed

How this relates to you...

Word stress patterns can differ according to dialect. One of the defining characteristics of Southern pronunciation is the placement of stress on the **first** syllable of words that are typically stressed on the **second** syllable in Standard American English. This is particularly true of many nouns. As you review the following examples, we recommend saying them aloud.

Southern American Pronunciation	Standard American Pronunciation
Po-lice	Po-**lice**
Ce-ment	Ce-**ment**
In-sur-ance	In-**sur**-ance

Below is a list of multi-syllabic words to help you practice applying word stress to the second syllable of a word. This list is not meant to be comprehensive. Rather, its purpose is to train your ear.

After familiarizing yourself with the concept, you'll be able to use your skills to listen to other Standard American English speakers. Your ultimate goal is to be able to identify other words that are personally challenging. When in doubt, a dictionary can be an excellent reference. Most break down words into stressed and unstressed syllables. Use the audio CD to listen to and repeat these words using Standard American English word stress.

Po-**lice**	Ju-**ly**
Ce-**ment**	Re-**peat**
De-**troit**	Um-**brell**-a
Be-**hind**	Se-**mes**-ter
Dis-**play**	Re-**cyc**-le
T-**V**	In-**sur**-ance
Gui-**tar**	Thanks-**giv**-ing

LESSON 25
"I RECKON WE BEST" ADDRESS
SOUTHERN GRAMMAR AND VOCABULARY:
A Review of Language Rules & Common Expressions

CAUTION: Rules Ahead!...

As previously mentioned, a "dialect" is compromised of sound pronunciation, lexicon, and grammar. Since grammar is a component of a dialect, let's review some of the grammatical structures distinctive to Southern speech.

Take some time to look over the information below. **Your goal is to avoid these Southern grammatical structures and to apply the suggested alternative.** This, of course, will take some time and practice, but familiarizing yourself with the rules is half the battle!

Grammatical Structure	Examples
Avoid: Using "got" to denote possession	"I got two eyes."
Alternative: Use "have" or "'ve got" to denote possession	"I have two eyes." "I've got two eyes."
Avoid: Using "them" as a demonstrative adjective replacing "those"	"Wipe down them tables."
Alternative: Use "those"	"Wipe down those tables."
Avoid: Using double modals	"I might could get there on time."
Alternative: Use single modals	"I could get there on time."

Avoid: Using "got to" to specify an action just beginning	"I got to talking to him."
Alternative: Use "started" or "began"	"I began talking to him." "I started talking to him."
Avoid: Placing the "a" sound before –ing verbs	"We're a-celebrating tomorrow."
Alternative: Leave off the "a"	"We're celebrating tomorrow."
Avoid: Using "don't" for "doesn't"	"Karen don't like coffee."
Alternative: Use "doesn't"	"Karen doesn't like coffee."
Avoid: Using "me," "him," "her," etc. as part of a reflexive verb	"I need to cook me some dinner." "She's going to buy her a new dress."
Alternative: Use "myself," "himself," "herself," etc. with reflexive verbs	"I need to cook myself dinner." "She's going to buy herself a new dress."
Avoid: Replacing multiple adjective forms in place of adverbs	"He hurt his foot real bad."
Alternative: Use the adverbial form	"He hurt his foot really badly."
Avoid: Using "seen" without "have"	"I seen her at church."
Alternative: Use "have seen" or "saw" to indicate past tense of "see"	"I have seen her at church many times." "I saw her at church yesterday."

Looky Here...

While addressing the Southern dialect, we must consider the lexical components of vocabulary and expressions. Lexicon is an identifying characteristic of any dialect. The minute a listener hears "y'all," they'll assume you're from the South.

To say there is a wide range of vocabulary and expressions unique to the Southern dialect would be a vast understatement! Different regions use their own variety of colorful expressions. Further, the expressions will differ from person to person within the same region. While it would be impossible to list all of the vocabulary and expressions used in Southern American English, the list on the next page provides a representative sampling.

We recommend that you:
1. Highlight the Southern vocabulary and expressions from the list that you use in your speech
2. Use the list to jog your memory and take note of other vocabulary and expressions you use that are not listed
3. Then, think of other ways you may express the same thoughts without putting a spotlight on your Southern heritage.

In conclusion, this list is meant to start you off on the right foot and get you used to coming up with new ways to phrase things. You should consider improving your lexicon a "work in progress." Start paying attention to your speech and the speech of others. Which phrases are distinctly Southern? And how else can you say them?

A Sampling of Southern Vocabulary & Expressions

ain't	holler
all covered up	hush your mouth
all get out	I do declare
awfully	kin
best (you best)	lick and a promise
bless your heart	looky here
britches	make like
carry on	mash the button
crank the car	mess of (to mean "a lot of")
critter	much obliged
cut off / on	pay no mind
cut up	pitch a fit
dang	reckon
dinner (to indicate lunch)	right quick
doohickey	ruckus
done told	running one's mouth
ever I saw	say what?
fetch	shut your mouth
fixin'	stompin' grounds
fuss	tore up
get me some	wore out
gracious me	y'all (and all y'all)
hissy fit	yonder
hog wild	young'un / youngin

Other Southern vocabulary and expressions that I use:

PHASE 4:
SUMMARY & GUIDELINES FOR FUTURE IMPROVEMENT

Congratulations on completing *Say Goodbye to Your Southern Accent!* We are honored to have been a part of your journey.

By this time, we expect that you have:

✓ Identified which region of the U.S. has influenced your Southern speaking patterns

✓ Sharpened your listening skills for both your own speech and the speech of others

✓ Used the text and audio CD to complete each target sound and content lesson that is applicable to your specific Southern dialect

✓ Mastered the Vowel Reduction Technique (VRT) and other techniques in all applicable target sounds

✓ Taken ample time to focus on carryover with each target sound and content chapter

✓ Gained complete confidence in your ability to use a Standard American English dialect in the words, sentences, and paragraph sections of the target sound lessons

✓ Achieved carryover of the Standard American English dialect at the conversational level

By now, some of you may have achieved carryover at the conversational level. Others may feel that using a Standard American English dialect is not quite effortless yet. If this is the case, be assured that you will get there with a little extra practice. If you feel like you need an added push to achieve carryover into conversational speech, start focusing on daily practice using the carryover suggestions in the "Fixin' to" Start the Program chapter on pages 5-11. Practice as much as you can. Over time, you'll find that you're using your new skills with ease.

In any case, on occasion, we recommend going back and reviewing the lessons that were especially challenging...

Ya'll come back now, ya hear?
(Or in Standard American English dialect:
Come back soon, okay?)

About Atlanta Accent Management

In 2002, Jennifer Adams and Johanna Chapman teamed up to form Atlanta Accent Management. Now Atlanta's premier provider of accent reduction services, the company is focused on providing exceptional and personalized accent reduction services. Jennifer and Johanna's proven methods and techniques have helped thousands of people improve their communication skills and increase their confidence. Clients have included professionals from major corporations, such as: Cingular, Coca Cola, DuPont, Emory University, Hyundai, Kimberly Clark Corporation, Lafarge North America, Nokia, SAP, Siemens, Solvay Pharmaceuticals, and Turner Broadcasting.

About Language Success Press

Language Success Press is a premier publisher of language books and multimedia materials. The publishing house offers a range of popular books and CDs to help achieve career success through mastery of standard, conversational American English.

Please visit the Language Success Press website at:
www.languagesuccesspress.com

ORDER FORM

TITLE	Quantity	Line Total
Say Goodbye to Your Southern Accent (Book & Audio CD)...$29.95		
Master the American Accent (Workbook, CD-ROM & 4 Audio CDs)...$79.95		
Lose Your Accent in 28 Days (Workbook, CD-ROM & Audio CD)...$49.95		
Speak English Like an American (Book & Audio CD) Select language version: ☐ all-English version ☐ for Chinese Speakers ☐ for Russian Speakers ☐ for Spanish Speakers ☐ for Japanese Speakers...$24.95		
More Speak English Like an American (Book & Audio CD)...$29.95		
Speak Business English Like an American (Book & Audio CD). Select language version: ☐ all-English version ☐ for Russian Speakers ☐ for Chinese Speakers...$29.95		
Say it Better in English...$24.95		
Subtotal		
Shipment to Michigan Add 6% Sales Tax		
Shipping (see below)		
TOTAL		

U.S. Shipping: $6.95 for orders up to $50. $7.95 for orders from $50.01 to $75. $9.95 for orders $75.01-$100. $11.95 for orders from $100.01-$200. Add an additional $4 for each additional $100 or part thereof. **International Shipping**: Multiply the U.S. shipping rate by 2.

Please charge my: ☐ VISA ☐ MASTERCARD ☐ AMERICAN EXPRESS

Card #_____ Expiration_____

Name on card_____

Ship to:

Name_____

Organization_____

Address_____

City_____ State_____ Zip_____ Country_____

Phone_____ E-mail_____

🖹 FAX this form to Language Success Press: 1-303-484-2004
🖰 ORDER ONLINE: www.languagesuccesspress.com
Language Success Press
2232 S. Main St #345
Ann Arbor, MI 48103